Living in Ancient Egypt

THE NEW KINGDOM

R J UNSTEAD

**Illustrated by
Ron Stenberg**

**A & C Black
London**

Living in . . .

a Castle	the time of the Pilgrim Fathers
a Crusader Land	the Elizabethan Court
a Medieval City	Samuel Pepys' London
a Medieval Village	Pompeii
Aztec Times	Ancient Egypt

First published 1977
A & C Black Ltd
35 Bedford Row
London WC1R 4JH

ISBN 0 7136 1713 6
© 1977 A & C Black Ltd

Printed and bound in Great Britain by
Morrison & Gibb Ltd, London and Edinburgh

Contents

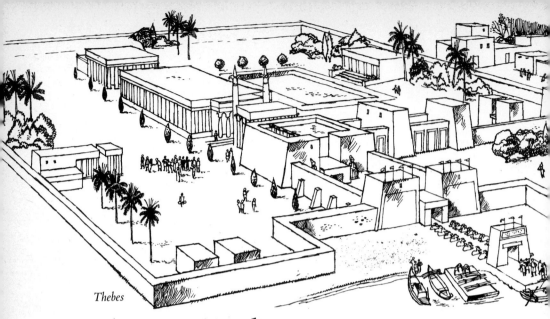

Thebes

The New Kingdom

The period known as the New Kingdom lasted from about 1560
B.C. to 1085 B.C. Egypt was already a very old civilization. The
pyramids near Memphis were over a thousand years old and the
capital had been moved from Memphis to Thebes, with its vast
temples of the god Amen-Ra. Warlike kings had conquered an
empire in Asia, and Egypt was at the zenith of its power and
influence.

At the head of all things stood Pharaoh, the king, who was con-
sidered to be a god, son of Ra, the sun-god. This divine ruler
owned all Egypt—its land, building-stone, gold, silver, and other
metals—and controlled foreign trade. His chief official was the
Vizier, whose duty was to fulfil Pharaoh's every wish. Under the
Vizier a huge class of officials carried out the business of running
the country. They supervised irrigation (the digging of canals and
watering of fields), collection of taxes, justice, measurement of the
harvest, counting of cattle, building projects, trading and mining,
levying troops and raising labour battalions for all the royal works.
These officials formed most of the educated class of the country,
from which came also the scribes and shaven-headed priests.

Responsible for Egypt's wonderful achievements in building and the arts were the thousands of craftsmen who handed on their skills from father to son—masons, sculptors, wall-painters, carpenters, goldsmiths and workers in precious stones. There were also leather workers, armourers and chariot-makers. At a humbler level came the potters and brick-makers who moulded the Nile mud and dried the bricks in the hot sunshine.

At the bottom of society, only just above the slaves captured in war, came the peasants. Ill-used by some masters, though cherished by others, they toiled in the fields to produce much of the wealth that enabled Pharaoh and the richest officials to live 'like gods'.

Slaves were not numerous until the period of the New Kingdom when foreign conquests brought many of them into Egypt. They seem to have carried out some of the tasks previously done by forced labour. According to the Old Testament, the Israelites were put to brickmaking.

The inundation

The people of the New Kingdom, like their ancestors, believed that every year in June the goddess Isis let fall a tear into the sacred waters of the Nile. This caused the river to rise until it overflowed its banks and spread far across the land to the edges of the desert on either side. (The true cause was heavy rainfall in the mountains of central Africa, to the south, but this was not known until centuries later).

By September, the country was a vast lake in which towns and villages stood out like islands, for each was protected by strong banks or dykes which had to be carefully watched and kept in repair. People could only get about by boat or along the raised roadways which were at other times the banks of irrigation canals.

During the inundation

As surely as they had risen, the waters began to subside and, by November, the river was back between its banks. Then peasants could start ploughing the rich mud that had been left behind in the fields.

This was *Peret*, the sowing season, when the sower walked ahead of the plough oxen and sheep might be driven across the fields to tread in the grain. After four or five months came *Shemu*, the harvest season, when the ripe grain was cut, threshed, winnowed and stored in brick granaries. Once in a while, the river failed to rise as high as usual, despite prayers to Isis. Since it hardly ever rained in Egypt, this meant a poor harvest, even famine.

By May, when the land was parched by the great heat and the Nile had dropped to its lowest level, everyone was waiting for the miracle to happen again—for Isis to shed her tear, so that the flooding, the *inundation*, would renew the land's fertility.

Farming

Although Egyptians never lost their fear of famine, Egypt was in most years a land of plenty, for the soil produced wonderful crops.

In theory, all the land belonged to the Pharaoh, but he gave estates to his relations, friends and chief officials, and some small patches to veteran soldiers. He also gave enormous estates to the temples.

In tomb-paintings, the master of an estate is often shown seated approvingly on a stool as the peasants file past, leading horned cattle and bearing baskets of grapes and other produce. Or he is shown watching the workers in the fields, the vineyard or on the threshing floor. The plough, like a large hoe with two handles, was pulled by a pair of oxen or donkeys; the sower carried seed in a bag and the reapers used curved sickles to cut off the ripe ears. Oxen trod out the grain which was winnowed by being tossed in the air with wooden shovels.

Main crops were barley and wheat, with a little millet. Cattle and sheep had to be fed mostly on grain and straw as the climate was generally unsuitable for pasture. Great quantities of flax were grown for linen, while papyrus, the reed used for boats, ropes, mats, sandals and writing-paper, grew mostly in the Delta. Vegetables grew quickly in the rich soil. They included onions, radishes, lettuces and gourds. Fruit also grew well: grapes, figs and dates were the commonest kinds.

To irrigate the land, farmers relied on water-basins and canals fed by the Nile. They also sank wells. For daily watering of vegetable gardens, the *shaduf* was invaluable, as it still is today. It is a bucket attached to a counter-weighted pole and, where the river bank is high, two or three *shadufs* on ledges raise the water into tanks and thence it is tipped into channels irrigating the gardens.

A shaduf

Food

Most people lived chiefly on cereal foods, fruit and vegetables, with an occasional meat dish made from lamb, kid or water-birds caught by snares set in the reeds. Fish from the sacred Nile were not supposed to be caught and eaten but, in practice, most people —especially the poor—ate a lot of fish. Nor were pigs supposed to be eaten or offered for sacrifice, yet the poor kept pigs and ate pork! It was probably only the royal family and the priests who avoided these 'forbidden' foods, for in the tomb of a wealthy woman archaeologists found the remains of Nile fish, and also stewed pigeon, ribs of beef, lamb's kidneys, a quail, bread, cakes and fruit.

Harvest-time

A nobleman hunting

The rich lived extremely well, eating a lot of beef and fowls of various kinds, such as geese, quails, cranes, pigeons and ducks—though the domestic cock and hen were unknown. They also enjoyed the flesh of wild animals which they hunted in the desert, principally antelopes, gazelles and oryx.

In the kitchen

Egyptians were great eaters of bread and cakes which were baked at home in a variety of shapes. The housewife ground barley or wheat herself, not in a handmill, since this was not yet in use, but with a sort of rolling pin on a sloping stone called a quern. She then added yeast and perhaps wild honey before kneading and baking the loaves in a brick oven. Bread was looked upon as *the* essential food and soldiers on campaign received a ration of about 4 lb a day. It was a coarse type of loaf as the flour contained a lot of grit, so that the soldiers are said to have worn their teeth down to the gums!

Salads and vegetable stews were much eaten; some experts say that beans and peas were forbidden, but they have been found in tombs. As well as grapes, figs and dates, apples and pomegranates grew well and coconuts were much prized. Oranges, lemons, bananas, pears and peaches were as yet unknown.

Food and drink were sweetened with honey gathered from wild bees in the desert or from domestic bees kept in pottery hives. Pods of the carob tree also provided sweetness and the poor chewed the sweet-tasting papyrus stalks.

The national drink was beer, made by treading barley bread in huge vats, adding a sweet liquor made from dates and leaving the mixture to ferment. The result was a beer almost as strong as wine to which the Egyptians, who loved merry-making, gave such names as 'The Joy-bringer' and 'The Heavenly'.

Date wine was popular, too, but grape wine was expensive: the grapes were trodden by peasants to the accompaniment of music or were squeezed by being wrung out in a linen bag slung between two posts. People seldom drank milk, which was looked on as a rare delicacy, and hardly ever ate butter or cheese. They used oil for cooking and also for cleaning and anointing their bodies— obtaining oil not from olives which did not flourish in Egypt, but from sesame, flax seeds and the castor oil plant.

Cooking was done in a pot on top of an earthenware stove about three feet high, or on a small metal stove. Birds and fillets of meat were roasted on spits. The main fuels were charcoal, dried papyrus roots, dried dung, chaff, mimosa and tamarisk wood.

Preparing for a banquet

Houses

Towns in Ancient Egypt were sited near the Nile or connected to it by canal. They usually stood on infertile spots because the rich soil was too precious to build on.

Inside the mud-brick town wall, houses of all kinds stood close together, crowding up to the very walls of the temple, whose massive entrance-towers, called *pylons*, dwarfed all other buildings. Only the temple was built of stone for, being the home of the gods, it was meant to last for ever. All the other houses were built of sun-dried mud bricks. Those of poorer people were erected in rows along streets no wider than an alley; their doors opened on to the street or on to a small yard with a tamarisk tree. Like peasant huts, they consisted of two or three rooms but each had an outside staircase leading to the flat roof which served as a sleeping place in hot weather and at times for cooking.

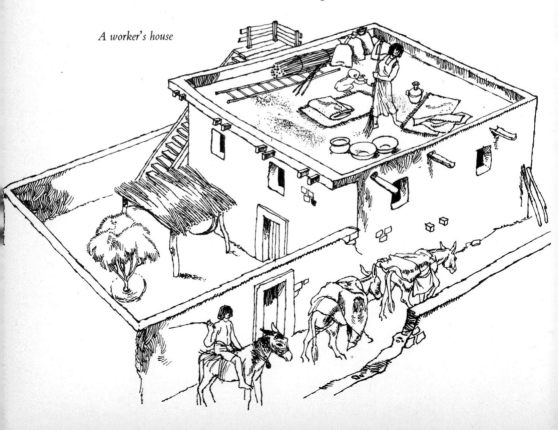

A worker's house

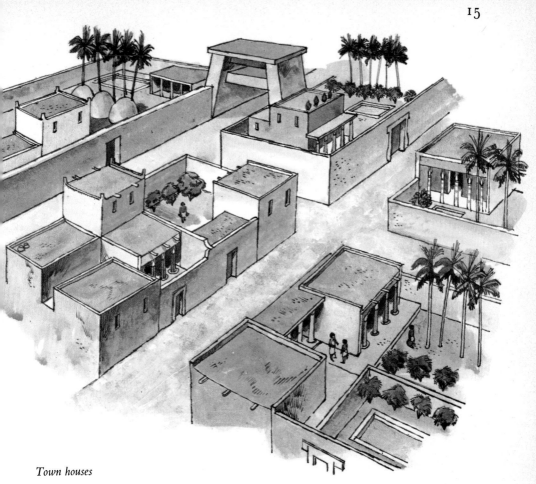

Town houses

The streets were kept clean and neat, and there were public gardens which provided townsfolk with a shady area in which to stroll and meet their neighbours.

A middle-class official's house was probably built in two or three storeys, with the ground floor reserved for household tasks, such as spinning, weaving, grinding corn, making bread and cooking. The first floor, with a verandah looking on to the street, contained the family's living-rooms which were lit by small windows fitted with latticed screens to keep the interior cool. The flat roof was used for sleeping and also as a storage for corn bins.

The villas of rich officials were much finer. Each stood in a handsome garden surrounded by a high wall, pierced by an imposing gateway. A visitor was conducted by a servant across a tree-fringed courtyard to the house which, with its portico of gaily painted lotus-shaped columns, looked like a small temple. Under this cool north-facing portico, he was greeted by his host and led into a large white-walled reception room whose ceiling, blue like the sky, was supported by four wooden pillars. There were rugs on the floor and colourful carpets or flower paintings on the walls.

Beyond the reception rooms and dining room lay the women's quarters (rich men usually had several wives), bedrooms, bathroom and lavatory. In the tiled bathroom, the master sat on a stone seat to be sluiced with water before a massage. Next door, the lavatory had a seat over a container filled with sand.

Behind this part of the villa stretched several courtyards containing the steward's house, servants' quarters, kitchen, bakehouse, stables and beehive-shaped corn bins. The whole establishment was managed by the steward, whose staff of servants included scribes, gardeners, vintners, carpenters, herdsmen, cooks and laundry-maids. Every villa had its own well. Egyptians loved gardens and took special care of trees, since they did not grow readily in the hot dry climate. The principal ones were date and coconut palms, acacia, yew, carob, tamarisk, sycamore fig, willow and pomegranate. No large garden was complete without its pool, ornamented with water-lilies and domestic ducks, or its little summer-houses, set amid the flowers and shrubs, where cool drinks were served to guests.

Furniture

It never occurred to the Egyptians to make large dining-tables. Master, mistress and guests would eat separately or in pairs at small circular tables, made of rare and costly timber. Very little native wood was suitable for carpentry, so the finest chairs were also made of valuable imported timber, with inlays of gold, ivory and mother-of-pearl. Some chairs had high backs and legs ending as lions' paws, while others were more like stools, with backs only a few inches high. The supports of folding stools might be carved to represent the heads of ducks or gazelles.

Beds consisted of a wooden frame with interlaced cord 'springs' and a mattress of folded sheets. In such a hot country, a neck-rest

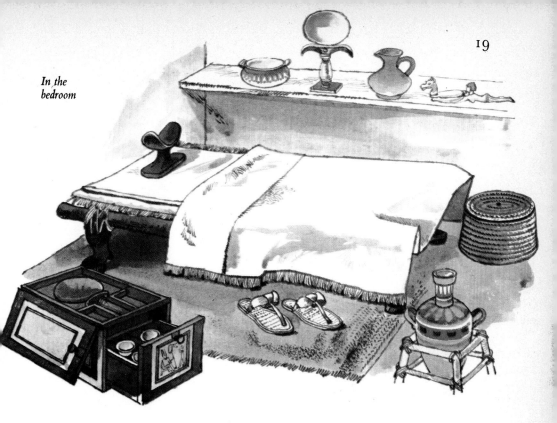

made of wood or alabaster was found to be more comfortable than
a soft pillow. Beds were sometimes made higher at the head than
the foot so that the sleeper lay in a sloping position.

Clothes and household linen were kept in wicker baskets and
wooden chests. Elaborate fitted boxes were made to contain
cosmetic sets, including mirror, razor and jars for rouge, eye-paint
and ointments.

Craftsmen acquired great skill in carving all manner of jugs,
bowls and vases out of stone, such as alabaster, rock crystal and
even granite. But the earthenware pottery was plain and rather
dull. Gold and silver plate came to be used by the rich while
poorer people made do with pottery and copper vessels.

A peasant's hut was furnished with a few sleeping mats, pots and
wooden boxes.

Dress

Thanks to the warm climate and absence of rain, people needed very little clothing. Young children ran about naked, while serving-maids and dancers wore little more than a girdle about their hips.

The chief material for clothing was linen, woven so fine that it was almost transparent. Nothing finer is made today. White was the favourite colour, though women's dresses were often coloured and sometimes embroidered with coloured threads or decorated with appliqué work.

Men of all classes wore a plain kilt, fastened by a girdle knotted in front; this simple garment became a little more complicated for important people, with the back longer than the front and part raised to show an under kilt. Well-to-do men also wore a short wide cape that hung from the shoulders to give the appearance of sleeves. A priest's dress was distinguished by the leopard skin he wore over one shoulder.

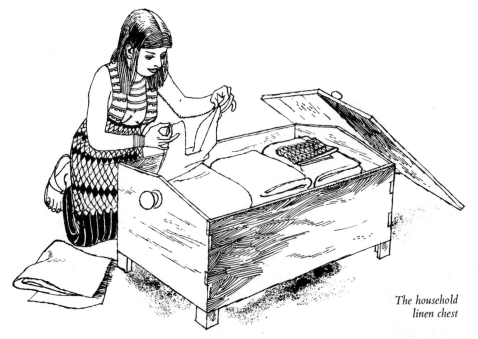

The household linen chest

A woman's basic dress was a close-fitting tunic that covered the body from neck to ankles. During the New Kingdom period fine narrow pleats were introduced. The dress might have short sleeves or be sleeveless with shoulder-straps and the right breast left bare. Two-piece costumes came in when the tunic was accompanied by a wide outer garment knotted over the breast and covering one arm; a short decorated cape might be added.

Egyptians generally went bare-headed, though upper-class men and women liked to wear elaborate wigs or linen scarves hanging behind the head. Women's hair was generally worn long, though rich women often had it cut short with a fringe. The Pharaoh wore a folded pleated head-dress reaching to the shoulders, as well as the Double Crown of Upper and Lower Egypt on ceremonial occasions.

Barbers did a good trade because Egyptian men were always clean-shaven—even the Pharaoh's ceremonial beard was a false one. Priests shaved the whole head.

Most people, even the rich, went barefoot. Sandals, made from papyrus, palm leaves or leather, were worn from time to time. They were carried around by a servant attending his master who would put them on when he arrived at his destination or received a visitor at home.

Both men and women loved jewellery of every kind—bracelets, anklets, rings, necklaces and elaborately beautiful pectorals. Earrings became popular in the New Kingdom period.

Rich ladies spent a great deal of time over their toilet, having their hair dressed by maids, their cheeks rouged with red ochre and their nails, the palms of their hands and soles of their feet reddened with henna. Nearly everyone wore eye-paint, black on the upper lids, green on the lower; sometimes each eye was given a complete black outline. Men, too, painted their eyelids. The paints may have given some protection against the eye infections so common in hot countries.

The Egyptians were fanatically clean people, washing several times a day and loving to anoint their bodies with oils made from animal fats, perfumed with flowers, seeds and aromatic gums. In a hot dry climate, these oils helped to keep the skin healthy and even soldiers and workmen insisted on having their ration of body oils.

The family

Egyptians were affectionate cheerful people. In paintings and sculptures, husbands and wives are often shown clasping each other's waist and caressing their children, who clamber on to their parents' knees or lovingly pat their faces.

Marriages were arranged, usually between teenagers. The husband provided the home, while the wife brought the dowry given by her father. In law, a woman was very much the equal of her husband; she was the mistress of the household and its goods belonged to her. However, the husband *was* entitled to beat his wife though he probably heeded a famous sage's advice: 'Love your wife. Feed her and clothe her and make her happy as long as you are alive ... keep her from getting the mastery.' From the start, a couple's greatest happiness was to have children.

After consulting astrologers to obtain the newborn child's horoscope to see if the future was to be lucky or ill-fated, parents chose the baby's name. They might call it after a god—Seti, for example, after Seth, Hori after Horus—or choose the name of a flower, tree or animal—'Wild Lotus', 'Little Lion' or 'Beautiful Kitten'—or simply something short like Ti, Abi, or To. Mothers were always worried about evil spirits who were supposed to be a danger to anyone asleep. Mothers tied a magic charm round the sleeping child's neck as a protection. Children shared fully in family life, accompanying their parents on outings and fishing expeditions, and attending grown-ups' parties.

Egyptians were very fond of family pets, especially cats, dogs and monkeys, and were clever at training them. They taught cats to retrieve birds and fish on hunting expeditions and pet monkeys to pick fruit. Rich homes quite often kept a dwarf or hunchback to amuse family and guests, rather like medieval jesters.

Family pets

Learning a trade

In many families, when a boy turned five he put away his toys and started to learn his father's trade. He might become a carpenter, learning in time how to use a hammer, saw, chisel and adze (a blade fixed to a handle to make a kind of plane). He found out how to make plywood and the beautiful inlays that decorated furniture and the boxes in which great ladies kept their hand mirror and jars of make-up.

Or the boy might be trained to become a glass-maker. Instead of blowing glass (a method not yet known), he heated quartz with natron (a kind of soda) and cast vases and statuettes, besides making *faience*, a lovely glaze for earthenware and jewellery.

He might follow his father as a fowler, snaring birds in the marshes, a sandalmaker, a coppersmith or a barber, who carried his block of wood for a customer to sit on while he shaved him in the open air.

A paper-maker sliced papyrus stalks into long strips, laid them side by side and laid another layer of strips across them on top. He poured water over the sheet and hammered it flat with a mallet before leaving it to dry in the sun. To make a roll or a 'book', he pasted several sheets together edge to edge.

Some boys became scribes. They had to go to school and live in dormitories, get up early for lessons, learn to do sums on the abacus, to draw letters and eventually to copy poems and religious verses. Life was hard and the master beat them but, by twelve, a good pupil could become a junior scribe. He went on to learn how to write business letters, bills, farm accounts and official notices. When he grew up, a scribe would join the envied class of officials who had important well-paid jobs, since Egyptians had a passion for writing everything down.

Girls were brought up to help their mothers at home and by the river, doing the laundry and carrying waterpots. Some would train as dancers and musicians.

Trading

In the market-place, where merchants, craftsmen and peasants set out their wares for sale, all trading had to be by barter, because the Egyptians never invented a system of coinage. Workmen were paid in food, beer and clothes; a man calculated his taxes in corn and cattle, while Pharaoh's wealth, piled high in storehouses throughout the land, consisted of grain, cloth, jewels and precious metals.

But, if they had no money, people knew the weight of metals, so, when they wanted to buy or sell something, they would agree that its value was so many *deben* (about 2½ oz) of gold, silver or copper. An ox, for example, was worth 100 *deben* of copper, so its owner might sell it for say, one fine gown worth 60 *deben*, plus ten sacks of wheat, a necklace and a basket of dried fish, together valued at 40 *deben*. Business deals of this kind naturally led to a great deal of argument, as well as work for the scribes.

All foreign trade was controlled by Pharaoh. He despatched expeditions to Sinai to obtain copper and turquoise, to the eastern desert and Nubia for gold and, via the Red Sea, to the Land of Punt (Somalia) to exchange weapons, tools, linen and jewellery for ebony, ivory, leopard skins, monkeys, myrrh and the gums needed for making perfumed oils. When Nubian traders came from central Africa to the southern town of Elephantine, they bargained, not with independent merchants, but with Pharaoh's officials. His fleets were fitted out for trade with Crete and eastern Mediterranean ports, especially Byblos, which supplied timber, especially cedarwood, for ships, furniture and buildings.

Travel

A great deal of traffic moved up and down the long river valley, as royal personages, officials of every kind, priests, pilgrims, artists, architects, craftsmen, traders, soldiers and sailors travelled on business or pleasure.

Around towns, rich men went short distances in a carrying-chair or palanquin carried by slaves, but most preferred to drive a smart two-horse chariot. Peasants driving their livestock or taking produce to market on donkeys used the roadways that ran along the canal banks formed above flood-level by earth dug from the canal.

But the main route for travellers was the Nile. Thousands of vessels served the busy towns along its banks and lined the quays, loading and unloading goods and passengers. Small ferry-boats were made of bundles of papyrus reeds bound together with cord and smeared with pitch. They carried a couple of oarsmen who, when going downstream, made extra use of the current by lashing a hurdle to the bow.

The Nile was a wonderfully convenient river, because the prevailing north wind helped sailing ships to move upstream and the current carried vessels downstream. Large ships were constructed of short planks laid edge to edge like bricks and bound together by cross-pieces held by stout thongs. Bow and stern curved up high out of the water and were joined by a taut rope; a cabin and the mast were placed amidships and, while the steersman steered with a single oar over the stern, the captain stood in the bows, sounding the depth with a long pole. The mast carried a single sail and oars were used for extra speed or when the wind dropped.

On the river were also to be seen great rafts which carried granite blocks or an obelisk, and flat-bottomed barges which contained corn, cattle, huge bundles of papyrus or piles of building stone.

Forced labour

Some of the New Kingdom Pharaohs, notably Rameses II, who reigned for 67 years, were fanatical builders of temples and monuments. To carry out these colossal works, the royal architects needed thousands of workers in addition to slaves. They were obtained by means of the same forced labour system that had built the pyramids centuries before.

In theory, everyone, except officials, was liable to serve but, in practice, forced labour meant peasants and artisans. During the three or four months of the *inundation*, when the peasant had little to do, he could be called away from his village to work in one of the gangs employed in hauling blocks of stone, excavating rock tombs or building vast brick ramps. In addition, the forced labour system provided workers for the harvest or for some big irrigation project.

The Egyptians never invented the pulley or scaffolding. All their huge buildings were raised by muscle power, aided by ropes, wooden levers and rollers. Masons would smooth the bottom of a stone block weighing several tons and the workers would haul it up a ramp to where the blocks already in position had been made slippery with water, so that the new block could more easily be levered into place. As the building rose, the ramp had to be raised, also, but it was completely cleared away when the building was finished.

Forced labour workers received pay in the form of bread, vegetables, dried fish and beer. On long-term projects, such as the building of Akhenaten's new city in honour of the god Aten, the workers were housed with their families in rows of little terrace houses which were probably better than peasants' huts, for their outlines, which can still be seen today, show that they consisted of an entrance hall, living-room, bedroom and kitchen.

Undoubtedly, a good deal of work was carried out by slaves, such as the Israelites, who may have been ill treated by brutal overseers. In general, however, it seems likely that the Egyptian peasants felt it was their duty to work loyally for their divine ruler and the all-powerful gods.

In the desolate Valley of the Kings, where the Pharaohs were buried, was a village for the workers who dug out and decorated the royal rock tombs. For generations, about 70 workmen lived there in mud-brick houses, son probably following father, with

their own priests and resident foreman. They worked all the year round, but received a holiday every eleventh day and several days off for religious festivals, when they went back to their village homes and to their wives and children. Their rations of bread, beer, beans, onions, salt, dried meat and water were taken out across the desert on donkeys. Sometimes Pharaoh rewarded them with a special issue of clothing, salt, wine and body oils. They actually formed their own workers' council and when, in Rameses III's reign, the rations failed to arrive for some reason, they dared to go on strike and march down the valley to put their case to a high official. 'We are hungry,' they said. 'We have no clothes, no oil, no fish, no vegetables. Send word to Pharaoh, our master, or the Vizier, our chief, so that we may get something to live on.'

This first recorded strike in history resulted in victory for the workers. Their demand for a month's rations (i.e. their wages) was immediately granted and no-one was punished afterwards.

Amusements

Children had quite a good time, for they were much loved. Those from well-off homes had plenty of toys—dolls made from wood or clay which would be dressed or painted, some with legs and arms which were moved by pulling a string. Favourite working models were crocodiles, cats, dogs and oxen whose jaws opened when a lever was pressed. There were also paint-boxes and dolls' furniture.

Older boys enjoyed gymnastics, wrestling, tug-of-war and obstacle races. Warlike games, with miniature axes, slings, bows and arrows, were always popular. Girls liked dancing best, though they also played a ball game in which players rode pick-a-back on their partner's back.

Games and toys

Playing senet

Indoors, grown-ups played *senet*, a game in which pieces were moved up and down an ivory board according to the cast of throw-sticks used like dice. The other side of the board might be used for 'Hounds and Jackals', a game in which pegs with carved heads were moved to the throw of knucklebones.

Out of doors, rich men loved fishing or fowling from a skiff amidst the tall papyrus reeds along the river. Accompanied on the day's outing by wife, children and servants, they netted birds or brought them down with a throwing-stick and let the hunting cat retrieve them from the reeds. Harpoons were used to spear the giant Nile carp and also for the dangerous sport of hunting the hippopotamus.

Hunting in the desert was reserved for Pharaoh and the most important men who went out with professional archers to decoy deer, wild oxen, ostriches, hyena and other creatures into an ambush where they were shot down or killed by greyhounds.

Banquets

There were few pleasures which the rich Egyptian loved more than giving a dinner party. After his servants had killed and jointed an ox, cleaned fish and plucked various birds, there would be tremendous activity in the kitchen, where the cooks prepared joints, roasts and stews, baked bread and cakes, while the head servant selected the best wines, beer and tableware.

After the host had greeted his guests and seen that they were seated, according to rank, men on one side of the room, women on the other, the banquet would begin with serving-girls taking round flowers and perfumed cones which guests placed on their heads. As the meal proceeded the cones gradually melted, so that hair and neck were drenched in sweet-smelling ointment.

As people ate, musicians played on a variety of instruments such as the harp, lute, oboe, double flute, zither, castanets and a sort of

At the banquet

rattle called a sistrum. Singers accompanied themselves by clapping their hands and, as the meal neared its end, dancers and acrobats, clad in nothing but girdles, came in to entertain the company. Dancing was watched by host and guests, never indulged in; it consisted chiefly of graceful postures and movements performed by slaves and professional dancers.

Meanwhile, wine and beer were passed round so freely that some of the guests would become quite drunk and have to be carried out by their friends. The rest took no notice but went on enjoying themselves, according to the words of a popular song which declared:

Spend the day merrily,
Follow your desire as long as you live!
Put myrrh on your head and clothe yourself in fine linen.
Put garlands on the body of your beloved!
Set music before your face . . .

Religion

The Ancient Egyptians believed that the world was created by Atum, who was also Ra or Re, the sun-god. He created himself, then Shu (air) and Tefnut (moisture) who together produced Geb (earth) and Nut (the sky goddess). Then came the divine family of Osiris, his wife Isis and his brother Seth. Seth murdered Osiris and cut up his body. Isis eventually put the pieces together and brought Osiris back to life, but he became god of the underworld—of the dead. Their son Horus triumphed over his wicked uncle Seth and reigned on earth. In his lifetime, every Pharaoh ruled as Horus and became Osiris when he died.

There were over 600 other gods and goddessess. Every town had its own local god who was often linked with Ra to seem more important—Amen-Ra, for example, who was originally Amen, the local god of Thebes.

Gods and goddesses could take on various shapes: here are Isis, Sobek, Horus and Osiris

Every aspect of life and death had its special god: there was, for example, Hathor, the much-loved goddess of music and happiness, Khons, the moon god, Ptah, the creator god of craftsmen, Seshat, the goddess of writing, and Min, who made the crops grow. People did not actually worship animals, but they held them in great honour because they were associated with the gods who were usually depicted with human bodies and the heads of birds or animals. Horus was falcon-headed, Hathor had the head of a cow and there was Bast, the cat goddess, Khnum, ram-headed, Bes, the dwarf with a lion's face, Sobek, the crocodile, Thoth, the ibis-headed god of wisdom and Anubis, jackal god of mummification. Live animals associated with the gods were kept in the temples, a sacred crocodile for example, ibises, cats and sacred bulls.

Everyone believed in a world to the West to which the good would go after death. It would be just like Egypt but, to reach it, the dead man had to pass through terrible trials. Eventually, he would reach Osiris and have his heart weighed by Anubis to see if his good deeds outweighed the bad. If he failed, the Devourer took him, but if he passed the test he went on to a life of happiness with the 'Westerners'.

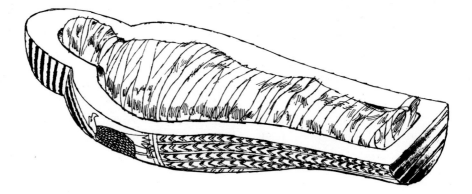

Because life would be the same in the next world, a man stored his tomb with as many splendid possessions as he could afford, and with food and drink for the long journey. Most important of all, he had to preserve his body, because it was the one to which his *Ka* or spirit would return. So, his dead body was specially treated by professional embalmers for 70 days and then wrapped in bandages adorned with magic charms, so that it became a mummy that would not decay. Sacred animals were mummified like human beings when they died. Even the poorest Egyptian was buried in a cloth wrapping and placed in a grave in the sand with some utensils and scraps of food.

As a mummy might be destroyed and all the riches and furniture stolen, the walls of the tomb had to be decorated with pictures of the dead man's everyday life on earth—by a magic process, these pictures would enable his spirit after all to live in the next world.

Because the Egyptians longed so dearly to enjoy the after-life, they had themselves buried in dry carefully hidden tombs. Yet practically every tomb was stripped by grave-robbers, apart from one belonging to the young Pharaoh, Tutankhamun. However, the tomb-paintings remain to tell us so much about life in Ancient Egypt.

Book list

The Pyramids, J. Weeks (Cambridge University Press)
Ancient Egypt, L. Casson (Time-Life)
Everday Life in Ancient Egypt, J. M. White (Batsford)
★Life under the Pharaohs, L. Cotterell (Evans)
The Egyptians: Pharaohs and Craftsmen, J. Van Duyn (Cassell)
How They Lived in Ancient Egypt, S. Hadenius & B. Janrup
(Lutterworth)
The Egyptians, A. Millard (Macdonald Educational)

★The title asterisked should still be available from libraries although it is out of print.

Index